This book belongs to

_____

This book is dedicated to my children - Mikey, Kobe, and Jojo.

Copyright © 2023 Grow Grit Press LLC. All rights reserved. No part of this book may be reproduced in any form without permission in writing from the publisher. Please send bulk order requests to info@ninjalifehacks.tv

Paperback ISBN: 978-1-63731-678-8
Hardcover ISBN: 978-1-63731-680-1
eBook ISBN: 978-1-63731-679-5

Printed and bound in the USA.
NinjaLifeHacks.tv

Ninja Life Hacks®
by Mary Nhin

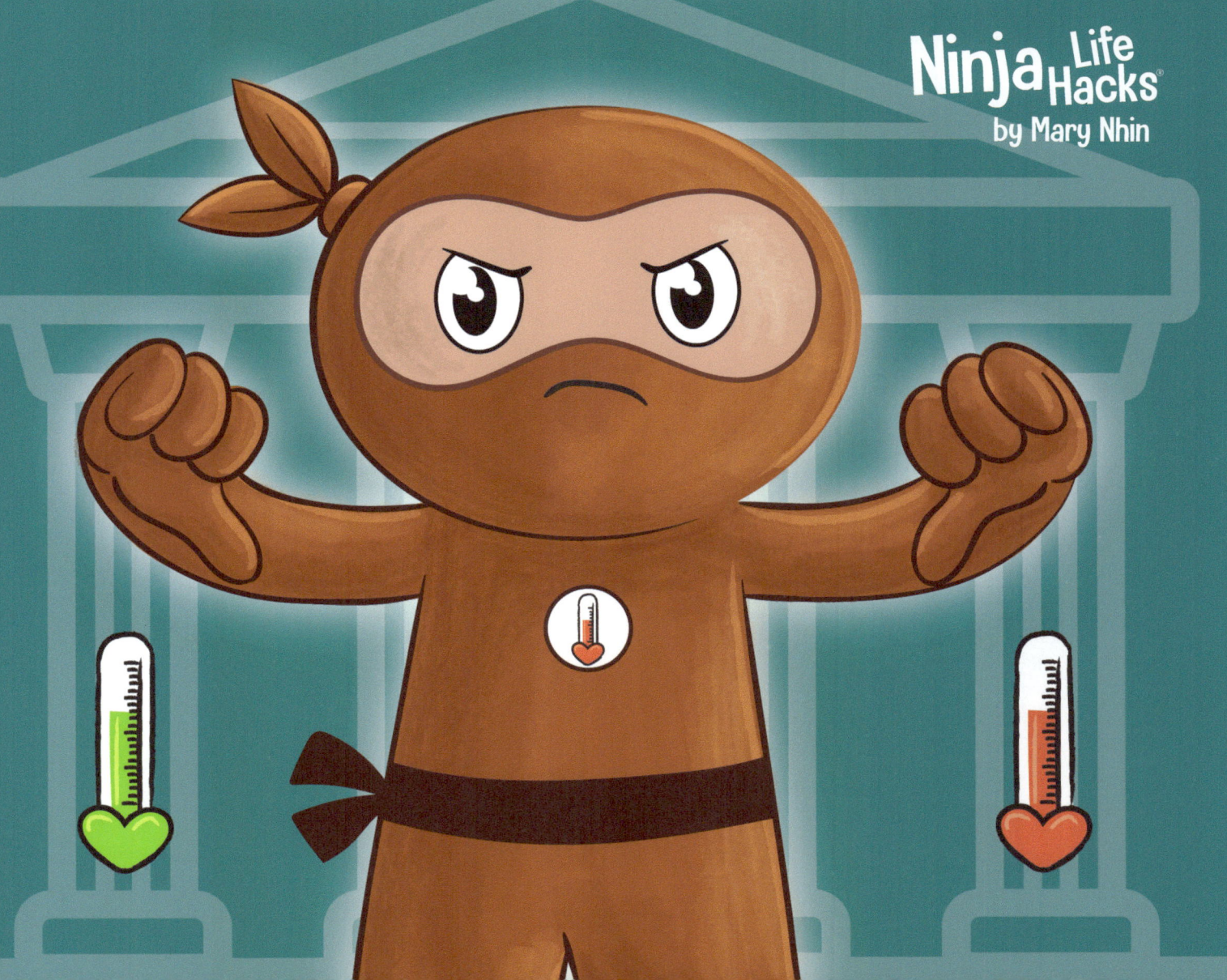

Remembering the Emotional Bank Account and the 3Ss could be your secret weapon in being less negative!

Check out the Negative Ninja lesson plans that contain fun activities to support the social, emotional lesson in this story at ninjalifehacks.tv!

I love to hear from my readers.
Write to me at info@ninjalifehacks.tv or send me mail at:

Mary Nhin
6608 N Western Avenue #1166
Oklahoma City, OK 73116